BY NADIA HIGGINS

Consultant:
Brett Barker, PhD
Associate Professor of History
University of Wisconsin–Marathon County

CAPSTONE PRESS
a capstone imprint

Fact Finders Books are published by Capstone Press,
1710 Roe Crest Drive, North Mankato, Minnesota 56003
www.capstonepub.com

Library of Congress Cataloging-in-Publication Data
Higgins, Nadia.
Last stand : causes and effects of the Battle of the Little Bighorn / by Nadia Higgins.
pages cm.—(Fact finders. Cause and effect: American Indian history)
Includes bibliographical references and index.
Audience: Grades 4-6.
ISBN 978-1-4914-2033-1 (library binding)
ISBN 978-1-4914-2208-3 (paperback)
ISBN 978-1-4914-2223-6 (ebook PDF)
1. Little Bighorn, Battle of the, Mont., 1876—Juvenile literature. 2. Dakota Indians—Wars—Juvenile literature. I. Title.
E83.876.H535 2015
973.8′2—dc23 2014033147

Editorial Credits
Catherine Neitge, editor; Bobbie Nuytten, designer; Eric Gohl, media researcher;
Morgan Walters, production specialist

Source Notes
Page 12, line 8: Connell, Evan S. *Son of the Morning Star: Custer and the Little Bighorn.* San Francisco: North Point Press, 1997, p. 274
Page 14, line 19: Marshall, Joseph M. *The Day the World Ended at Little Bighorn: A Lakota History.* New York: Viking, 2006, p. 1.
Page 15, line 10: "Battle of the Little Bighorn." Ranger Steve Adelson. C-Span Cities Tour–Billings. 4 Oct. 2013. 18 Sept. 2014. https://www.youtube.com/watch?v=q2UzKRUgzJ0
Page 18, line 6: Powers, Thomas. "How the Little Bighorn Was Won." *Smithsonian.* November 2010, pp. 82-106.
Page 18, line 15: Philbrick, Nathaniel. "Undying Fame." *American Heritage.* Spring 2010, pp. 26-37.
Page 18, line 23: Buchholtz, Debra. *The Battle of the Greasy Grass/Little Bighorn: Custer's Last Stand in Memory, History, and Popular Culture.* New York: Routledge, 2012, p. 65.

Photo Credits
Alamy: INTERFOTO, 28; Bridgeman Images: © Chicago History Museum, USA/Cross, Henry H. (1837-1918), 29 (top left), Private Collection/Lorenz, Richard (1858-1915), 5; Corbis: 23, Bettmann, 9, National Geographic Society/W. Langdon Kihn, 13; CriaImages.com: Jay Robert Nash Collection, 29 (top right & bottom right); Getty Images: The LIFE Picture Collection/National Archives/Time Life Pictures, 8, Print Collector/Ann Ronan Pictures, 15, 25; Library of Congress: cover, 10, 18, 21, 29 (middle right); Newscom: akg-images, 29 (bottom left), Everett Collection, 16, 24, World History Archive, 22; Shutterstock: Audrey Snider-Bell, 27, Zack Frank, 26; Wikimedia: Museum of the American Indian, 19, Public Domain, 11, 29 (middle left), Smithsonian American Art Museum, 7; World Book, Inc.: 17 (Historical Map: *The Battle of the Little Bighorn.* From: Urwin, Gregory J.W. "Little Bighorn, Battle of the." World Book Student. © 2014 World Book, Inc. By permission of the publisher. All rights reserved. This map may not be reproduced in whole or in part in any form without prior written permission from the publisher. www.worldbookonline.com)
Design Elements: Shutterstock

Printed in Canada.
102014 008478FRS15

Table of Contents

A LAST STAND

The Battle of the Little Bighorn was one of the most shocking military defeats in U.S. history. Lieutenant Colonel George A. Custer and more than 200 of his men died June 25, 1876. They were killed in a battle with American Indian warriors in southeastern Montana.

Long known as "Custer's Last Stand," the battle is rarely called that today as historians consider the Indian viewpoint. If anything, the battle represents the last stand of the Lakota Sioux nation. Along the Little Bighorn River, the native people defended their encampment and way of life. The Battle of the Greasy Grass, as they call it, was one of the greatest Indian victories ever. It was also one of their last.

What caused this famous battle? Whom did it affect, and how? The events of that distant summer day still echo in our own time.

The Battle of the Little Bighorn was a decisive victory for American Indians.

What Caused the BATTLE OF THE LITTLE BIGHORN?

In 1876 hostility ran deep between the U.S. government and American Indians. At its heart was a conflict over land.

Cause #1: The Struggle for Land

In the 1840s Americans viewed the **Great Plains** as a vast, empty land of promise. Pioneers in wagon trains began rolling in. Next came the gold miners. Railroads and military forts soon followed. White Americans believed that conquering the frontier was their "**Manifest Destiny**," their God-given right.

To the Plains Indians, that "destiny" looked more like greed. For generations the Indians survived by hunting buffalo. Their outrage grew as more newcomers invaded their hunting lands.

The U.S. government sought to solve the "Indian problem" by moving the native people to **reservations**. Native chiefs signed hundreds of **treaties** setting aside Indian land. As more settlers crowded in, the U.S. government broke those treaties.

Starting in 1854 several bloody clashes broke out between Lakota warriors and U.S. soldiers. Soon one attack led to another, and revenge became its own battle cry.

An 1861 mural representing Manifest Destiny hangs in the U.S. Capitol in Washington, D.C.

FAST FACT:

In the mid-1800s the U.S. population numbered about 25 million. In contrast, about 20,000 people belonged to the Lakota nation. Other Plains Indians included the Arapaho, Blackfeet, Cheyenne, Comanche, Crow, and Pawnee.

Great Plains—the broad, level land that stretches eastward from the base of the Rocky Mountains for about 400 miles (644 kilometers) in the United States and Canada

Manifest Destiny—the belief that God gave white Americans the right to take over North American land that belonged to other people

reservation—an area of land set aside by the U.S. government for American Indians; in Canada reservations are called reserves

treaty—an official agreement between two or more groups or countries

Cause #2: A Gold Rush and a Broken Treaty

Hard times fell on the United States in 1873. Many men were out of work. Rumors spread that the Black Hills of South Dakota were full of gold, just waiting for the taking. Army Lieutenant Colonel George A. Custer led an **expedition** into the hills in 1874 and reported that the rumors were true.

"Gold!" Across the country newspaper headlines celebrated Custer's find. But that news was anything but welcome for the Lakota. For them, the Black Hills were Paha Sapa, The Heart of Everything That Is. The sacred hills were protected Lakota land under the Treaty of Fort Laramie, signed in 1868.

U.S. President Ulysses S. Grant made an offer to buy the hills. Lakota holy ground was not for sale, chief Sitting Bull replied. Soon **prospectors** started streaming in anyway. Grant turned to his War Department for a way to seize the Black Hills.

More than 100 wagons in Custer's expedition snaked through the Black Hills.

Custer (seated) and Crow scouts in the early 1870s

About 50 Indian scouts helped Custer find his way through the plains. Many were from the Arikara and Crow nations. They were ancient enemies of the Lakota.

expedition—a group of people on a trip with a specific purpose, such as finding gold
prospector—person who looks for valuable minerals, especially silver and gold

Cause #3: A Threat Defied

The War Department issued an order—all Lakota people were to relocate onto their reservation by the end of January 1876. U.S. agents ran the reservation where Indians were forced to live. The army would round up all those found outside its borders.

This was taken as a declaration of war. According to the treaty, Lakota had the right to hunt buffalo outside of the reservation. Grant's generals knew Sitting Bull would never accept such a demand.

Sitting Bull told his people to take their freedom while they could. Lakota started pouring off the reservation to join him. Cheyenne Indians joined as well. Sitting Bull's band of followers grew to about 8,000 people. By June a huge camp had gathered by the Little Bighorn River. It included about 1,500 to 2,000 warriors. The Indian allies wanted peace, but they were prepared for war.

Sitting Bull posed for a formal photo in 1884.

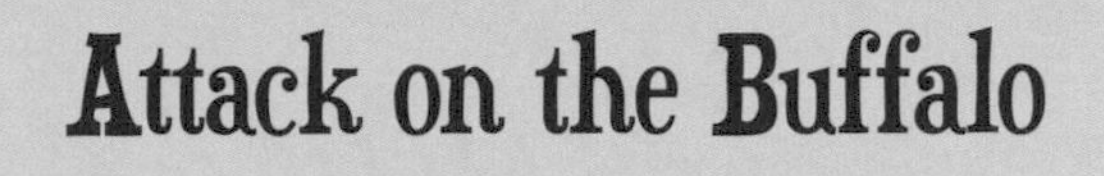

Attack on the Buffalo

In the early 1870s, millions of buffalo thundered over the Great Plains. Several Indian nations, including the Lakota, relied on the huge, shaggy animals for food, clothing, teepees, tools, and more.

The U.S. government understood that the best way to break the Plains Indians was to destroy the buffalo. Starting in the 1870s, the army sponsored buffalo hunts from open trains. Buffalo were killed for sport and for their tongues and hides. The huge animals were left to rot where they fell. In the East new methods were developed for tanning buffalo hides. Buffalo fur became very fashionable.

By 1884 only 325 buffalo were left on the plains. By then, all the Plains Indians lived on government-run reservations. Today the buffalo has recovered from near **extinction**.

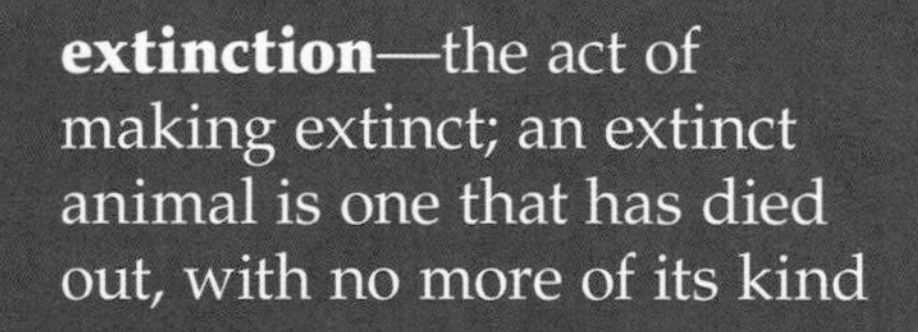

extinction—the act of making extinct; an extinct animal is one that has died out, with no more of its kind

A huge pile of buffalo skulls were ground into fertilizer in the mid-1870s.

Bloodshed ON THE PRAIRIE

Lieutenant Colonel George A. Custer and 650 men of the 7th **Cavalry** were hot on the trail of Sitting Bull's band. It was dawn June 25, 1876. The soldiers had been riding all night. Now Custer's Indian scouts pointed to what looked like worms squirming in the valley below. Those were grazing horses, and their sheer number told of a mighty force.

A scout, Half Yellow Face, warned Custer of a deadly outcome. He said, "You and I are both going home today by a road that we do not know."

cavalry—soldiers who fight on horseback

A huge encampment next to the Little Bighorn River included more than 1,500 warriors.

But Custer had a greater worry. He feared that the Indians would scatter before he could attack. He had orders to wait for more troops. But Custer wanted to earn fame before higher-ranking officers arrived. Also, the Civil War hero had not become famous by backing away.

"Onward!" Custer ordered. A few hours later, he split his men into three groups to surround the encampment. Major Marcus A. Reno would lead one group west across the river. Captain Frederick W. Benteen would lead his group southwest. Custer and his five companies headed north along the river bluffs.

First Charge

Meanwhile, the Indian villagers were going about their daily chores. It was an especially hot and muggy day. Many children were swimming in the river.

The news of Reno's approach jolted the village into action. Mothers ran to get their children. Warriors as young as 14 raced to grab their weapons. They put on war paint and mounted their horses.

Then something strange happened. Reno and his men suddenly halted outside the village. Sitting Bull wondered if the officers were coming to make a deal. He sent his nephew and another warrior to find out.

In truth, Reno was reacting to the village's huge size. U.S. soldiers were trained to fight with guns, from a distance. Indian warriors were good at hand-to-hand combat. Reno didn't want to get trapped inside the Lakota camp. He ordered his men to dismount, form a line, and fire.

The bullets rained down on the camp. Two wives and three daughters of chief Gall were shot down. The furious chief fought back "like a wounded bear," he later said.

Starting in about 1890, Amos Bad Heart Bull drew the history of his people, the Oglala Lakota. One of his drawings depicts Reno's men trying to escape across the Little Bighorn River.

"Hokahey!" Charge! Gall and his warriors galloped out of camp. The Lakota came at the soldiers with clubs, arrows, tomahawks, and guns. Bullets sent leaves fluttering to the ground near the river.

The Lakota were expert horsemen. And unlike the soldiers, they stayed mounted as they battled, sometimes hanging off the horse's side with one arm and leg. They fired their weapons from underneath their horses' necks.

Within 20 minutes Reno and his men were running for their lives. The warriors gave chase across the river. "We mowed the soldiers down. It was like a buffalo hunt," Cheyenne chief Two Moons would later recount. By the end of that first charge, almost half of Reno's men were killed, wounded, or missing. The Little Bighorn River turned red with blood.

Calhoun Hill

The survivors from Reno's group took up a defensive position on a nearby hill. Benteen's group returning from the south joined them. To the north, Custer heard news of Reno's defeat. He sent word to Benteen for help, but Benteen stayed put. Benteen did not like Custer. And he realized the seriousness of the situation and Custer's recklessness. Benteen would stay in his own superior defensive position and ignore Custer's request until it was too late.

Already, Indian forces were closing in on Custer. On Calhoun Hill, a new battle began. Now the Indians used guns taken from Reno's fallen troops.

Some of the U.S. soldiers fired back from their positions. Other soldiers had the job of holding the horses. In one key move, the Indians attacked the horse handlers. Then the warriors sent the horses stampeding away. Without horses, the soldiers would no longer be able to charge or flee. Their saddlebags with **ammunition** were also gone.

Indian warriors overpowered Custer's soldiers.

At one point, both sides kept low amid the noise and confusion. A **standoff** developed. Then, out of the smoke, Crazy Horse appeared. The famous Lakota warrior led charges on horseback, his eagle bone whistle shrieking. He and his warriors overwhelmed the soldiers.

ammunition—bullets
standoff—a point in battle when neither side is winning

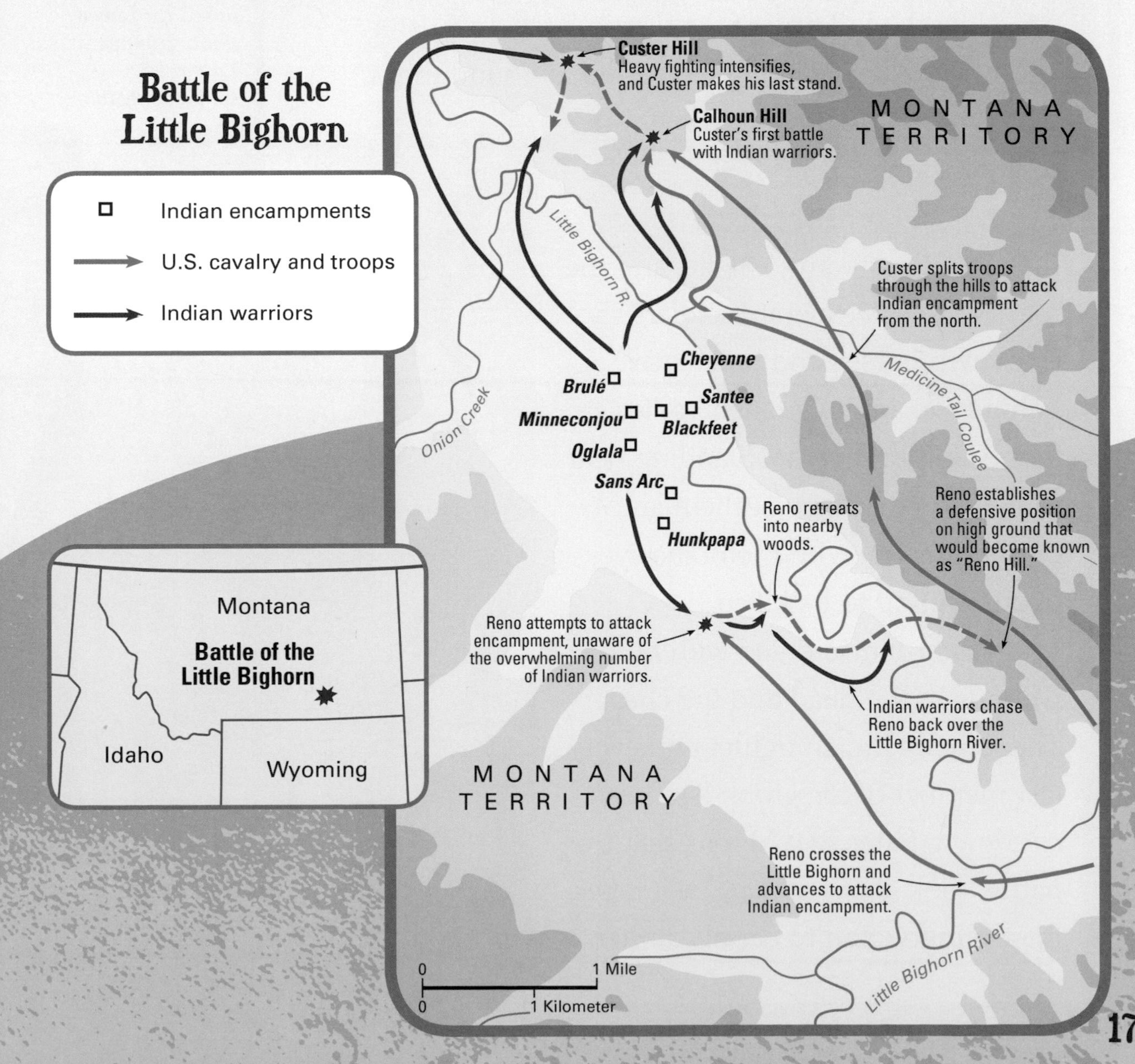

Last Stand Hill

Soon more than half of Custer's men were dead. The survivors from Calhoun Hill started fleeing on foot. They rushed toward the rest of their group on what is now called Last Stand Hill or Custer Hill.

Now the full fury of the warriors fell on Custer and his remaining men. "We circled all round them," Two Moons said, "swirling like water round a stone."

A final horrifying battle filled the air with screams, smoke, and the roar of guns. Desperate soldiers shot their own horses and took cover behind the animals' fallen bodies. Some simply gave up. Standing Bear remembered, "Many of them lay on the ground, with their blue eyes open, waiting to be killed."

Custer himself died with bullet wounds in the head and the chest. The famous Indian fighter and every last member of his group had been cut down. Later Two Moons said the battle "took about as long as it takes for a hungry man to eat his dinner."

Cheyenne chief Two Moons posed for famed photographer Edward S. Curtis in 1910.

Trapped by Sharpshooters

The remaining 350 men at Reno Hill had heard the battle 4 miles (6 km) away. But they could not join in. Indian sharpshooters trapped the soldiers through the long, hot night and into the morning.

In the afternoon the Lakota left. The defeated soldiers were no longer a threat. Sitting Bull had allowed them to leave to spread the news of the Indian victory.

Meanwhile, the Lakota received word that more soldiers were on their way. The Indians packed up their village and headed south. As they traveled the Lakota sang sounds of **mourning** for the 60 or so warriors who had died. They shared stories of the Battle of the Greasy Grass.

A buffalo hide painting from the late 1870s tells the story of the battle.

mourning—the act of showing sadness for the death of a loved one

What Effects Did the BATTLE OF THE LITTLE BIGHORN HAVE?

The Battle of the Little Bighorn did not last long, but it had deep, lasting effects.

Effect #1: Total War

News of the bloody battle reached the East at almost the exact moment of the country's 100th birthday, July 4, 1876. Americans were celebrating 100 years of progress and the "taming" of the West at the Centennial Exposition in Philadelphia. It was the first U.S. world's fair. Custer's shocking defeat outraged the nation. President Grant pushed through actions Congress had been too cautious to approve before. Soldiers flooded into the West. A policy of "total war" was pursued.

The U.S. army starved the Lakota. U.S. troops destroyed camps, killed buffalo, and burned prairie grasses. By spring 1877 almost all the Lakota were living on the reservation. This land itself had been reduced to one-sixth its original size. The United States seized the Black Hills outright—in direct violation of the Treaty of Fort Laramie.

End of a Way of Life

For generations the Lakota had hunted their own food. They had made their own bowls, knives, clothes, blankets, and housing. On the reservation they were forced to rely on the government for all these necessities. Their religious ceremonies were also outlawed.

Children were sent away to be raised like white Americans. At boarding school the boys were forced to cut their hair and wear white American-style clothing. Any child caught speaking Lakota was punished. Many children didn't see their families for years, and many died.

U.S. policy was to reshape the Lakota in the white man's image, but the Lakota adapted. Though much has been lost, they have survived to pass on their traditions.

A photographer in South Dakota titled his 1891 photo of Lakota "a pretty group at an Indian tent."

Effect #2: Fallen Chiefs

U.S. soldiers hounded Crazy Horse for months. On the brink of starvation, he surrendered in May 1877. Officials still viewed the warrior as a threat, though. The next September Crazy Horse left the reservation without permission. He was arrested and killed while being taken to a cell.

Custer and Crazy Horse do battle in a painting by Oglala Lakota artist Kills Two (Nupa Kte) (1869–1927)

Sitting Bull led a band of followers to Canada. But they too faced starvation and sickness. In July 1881 Sitting Bull surrendered. He was the last Lakota chief to do so. About 10 years later officials feared that the powerful leader was stirring unrest among his people. A **skirmish** broke out in December 1890, and Sitting Bull was killed by reservation police.

skirmish—a small fight that lasts for a brief time

Sitting Bull and his family pose for a photo with a cavalry officer's wife and daughter after the Lakota chief's surrender. A cavalry captain watches over.

Effect #3: The Myth of Custer

A popular writer, Frederick Whittaker, published a book about Custer's life in 1876. In this glowing report, Custer was a hero. He had bravely died for the cause of American progress. That view of Custer took hold among Americans. In addition, Custer's widow, Elizabeth Bacon Custer, spent her life defending her husband's honor and reputation. She wrote three books and gave lectures around the world glorifying Custer. Well into the 1950s, children pretended to be Custer in the game of "Cowboys and Indians."

An 1899 image put Custer at the center of the battle.

Historians took a more critical view. For decades they debated what Custer did wrong. He rushed into action. He shouldn't have split his troops. He should have turned back. The Lakota's greatest victory was a story about Custer's troubles. Today historians consider the Indian point of view.

Amos Bad Heart Bull's drawings focus on the Indian victory and their point of view.

Effect #4: Sacred Ground

The battle site became a tourist destination in 1879. It was called Custer Battlefield National Cemetery. A stone monument displayed the names of the fallen soldiers.

Starting in the 1970s American Indians started to reclaim this sacred site. Activists with the American Indian Movement held protests on the prairie bluffs. The name was changed to Little Bighorn Battlefield National Monument in 1991. An Indian memorial was added in 2003.

The Peace Through Unity Indian Memorial was unveiled on the 127th anniversary of the battle.

Each year about 400,000 people visit this national park. Lakota groups come to **reenact** the battle. They also perform religious dances and have meetings. They hold the memory of their nation's final stand close to their hearts.

Custer National Cemetery is part of the Little Bighorn Battlefield National Monument.

reenact—to act out something that happened in the past

Cause and Effect: Won the Battle, Lost the War

Sitting Bull's warriors won the Battle of the Little Bighorn, but they lost the war to save their nation. The U.S. military's shocking defeat on June 25, 1876, became a rallying cry for total war against the Lakota people. For years George Armstrong Custer was remembered as a fallen hero. Today the Lakota are reclaiming their past and the memory of the Battle of the Greasy Grass.

An 1890 painting depicts life on the Standing Rock Reservation. It straddles the borders of North and South Dakota.

WHO'S WHO

Frederick W. Benteen (1834-1898)
Career Army officer who ignored Custer's command for assistance, believing it would be disastrous for his men. Benteen had served in the Union Army during the Civil War.

Crazy Horse (1844?-1877)
Legendary Oglala Lakota war chief who worked to save his people's traditional way of life. He continued to resist, pursuing Army soldiers until his surrender in May 1877. He was killed while under arrest at Fort Robinson, Nebraska.

George Armstrong Custer (1839-1876)
Flashy Army officer who finished last in his class at the U.S. Military Academy but went on to serve well in the Civil War. Custer's stunning defeat at the Battle of the Little Bighorn sent shock waves across the nation.

Gall (1840-1894)
Hunkpapa Lakota war chief who served with Sitting Bull in many battles against the U.S. Army. Gall led his band to safety in Canada after Little Bighorn but returned to the U.S. in 1880. He became a farmer and supporter of reservation life.

Marcus A. Reno (1834-1889)
Ill-fated leader of the initial attack against the Indian village who was later charged with being a coward. He was cleared of the charge but forced out of the Army on unrelated charges in 1880. Nearly 100 years later a military court cleared Reno's name. He was reburied at Custer National Cemetery.

Sitting Bull (1834?-1890)
Fearless Hunkpapa Lakota chief and spiritual leader who united Lakota tribes to resist western expansion. Following the victory at the Little Bighorn, he led his band to safety in Canada but surrendered four years later. He was killed by reservation police in Dakota Territory.

GLOSSARY

ammunition (am-yuh-NI-shuhn)—bullets

cavalry (KA-vuhl-ree)—soldiers who fight on horseback

expedition (ek-spuh-DI-shuhn)—a group of people on a trip with a specific purpose, such as finding gold

extinction (ik-STINGKT-shun)—the act of making extinct; an extinct animal is one that has died out, with no more of its kind

Great Plains (GRAYT PLANES)—the broad, level land that stretches eastward from the base of the Rocky Mountains for about 400 miles (644 km) in the United States and Canada

Manifest Destiny (MAN-uh-fest DESS-tuh-nee)—the belief that God gave white Americans the right to take over North American land that belonged to other people

mourning (MORN-ing)—the act of showing sadness for the death of a loved one

prospector (PROSS-pekt-or)—person who looks for valuable minerals, especially silver and gold

reenact (ree-uh-NAKT)—to act out something that happened in the past

reservation (rez-er-VAY-shuhn)—an area of land set aside by the U.S. government for American Indians; in Canada reservations are called reserves

skirmish (SKUR-mish)—a small fight that lasts for a brief time

standoff (STAND-awf)—a point in battle when neither side is winning

treaty (TREE-tee)—an official agreement between two or more groups or countries

READ MORE

Collins, Terry. *Into the West: Causes and Effects of U.S. Westward Expansion*. North Mankato, Minn.: Capstone, 2014.

Goble, Paul. *Custer's Last Battle: Red Hawk's Account of the Battle of the Little Bighorn, June 25, 1876*. Bloomington, Ind.: Wisdom Tales, 2013.

Josephson, Judith Pinkerton. *Who Was Sitting Bull? And Other Questions about the Battle of Little Bighorn*. Minneapolis: Lerner, 2011.

Stanley, George E. *Sitting Bull: Great Sioux Hero.* New York: Sterling, 2010.

INTERNET SITES

FactHound offers a safe, fun way to find Internet sites related to this book. All of the sites on FactHound have been researched by our staff.

Here's all you do:

Visit *www.facthound.com*

Type in this code: 9781491420331

Check out projects, games and lots more at
www.capstonekids.com

CRITICAL THINKING USING THE COMMON CORE

1. Indian warriors used a different style of battle from the U.S. cavalry. What was one key difference, and how did it benefit the native fighters? (Key Ideas and Details)
2. The chapter "Bloodshed on the Prairie" directly quotes several Indian leaders. Many of the quotes are similes—poetic comparisons of one thing to another. Find at least two. How do the similes make the description more vivid? (Craft and Structure)
3. Historians have an obligation to critique and revise accepted stories about past events. In the case of "Custer's Last Stand," they incorporated the American Indian point of view and even changed the battle's name. Can you think of other stories from U.S. history that have been changed as new information and points of view have been considered? (Integration of Knowledge and Ideas)

INDEX

Causes and Effects of the Battle of the Little Bighorn

Americans remember the Battle of the Little Bighorn as Custer's Last Stand. But the shocking defeat of U.S. forces in 1876 represents the last stand of the Lakota nation. The greatest American Indian victory ever would be one of their last. How would it affect their lives and change the United States?

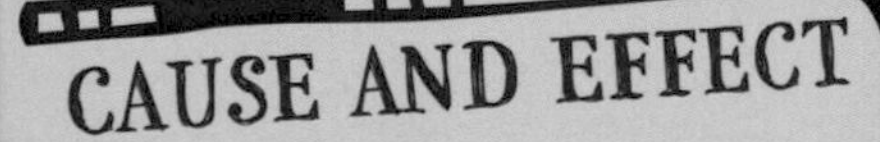

History is more than just our past. Decisions made long ago affect us even today. Explore the causes leading up to major events in American Indian history. Then examine their lasting effects on people and places.

Titles in this set:

DEFENDING THE LAND:
Causes and Effects of
Red Cloud's War

LAST STAND:
Causes and Effects of the
Battle of the Little Bighorn

FORCED REMOVAL:
Causes and Effects of
the Trail of Tears

SEEKING FREEDOM:
Causes and Effects of the
Flight of the Nez Perce

RL: 3-4 IL: 3-6

a capstone imprint
capstoneclassroom.com